THE
HABITAT GARDEN
BOOK

Wildlife Landscaping
for the San Francisco Bay Region

Nancy Bauer

First Edition
March 2001

THE
HABITAT GARDEN
BOOK

Wildlife Landscaping
for the San Francisco Bay Region

Library of Congress Catalog Card Number: 2001086272

ISBN: 0-9707445-0-1

Cover Photo: Anise Swallowtail, Louise Hallberg, Hallberg Butterfly Gardens, Sebastopol, California

Book Design & Production by Rita Ter Sarkissoff, Spring Hill Press, Sebastopol, California

Photo Credits:
All photographs by author except:
pp 2-3 (butterflies; Monarch caterpillar) Louise Hallberg; p8 (Buckeye) Yulan Tong; p9 (Strawberry Tree) Katherine Greenberg; pp10 (Ceanothus, Ribes), 11 (Buckwheat), 14 (Seaside Daisy), 15 (Dutchman's Pipe), 17 (Blue Oat Grass), 25 (Toyon), 27 (Ribes, Dogwood), 28 (Columbine), 33 (Ribes), 48 (apples) Judy Adler; p32 (poppy) Michel Ter Sarkissoff; pp37, 44 (ladybug) Don Mahoney; pp40-41 (dragonflies) Kathy Biggs
Printed in Korea

Coyote Ridge Press
P.O. Box 192
Sebastopol, CA 95473-0192
Email: nbauer@earthlink.net

For Maya and Nina

Today's children, growing up on lawns and pavements, will not even have nostalgia to guide them, and soon the animals will be not only missing, but forgotten.

SARA STEIN, *NOAH'S GARDEN*

INTRODUCTION

Creating Sanctuary

Memories of a favorite childhood garden inspired me to plant for butterflies, my first attempt at habitat gardening. My aunt's garden was a magical place from spring right into the crisp midwestern autumn. It was a tangle of fragrant flowers, patches of grassy weeds to hide in, hanging vines and violets, the sweetest purple grapes. Bees, fireflies, toads, caterpillars, and squirrels were just a few of the players on that garden stage.

A buzzing mini-ecosystem existed and thrived in that diverse, carefree garden. It created a vibrant and flowing harmony, as much felt as seen, that was far more attractive than the empty clipped hedges, lawns, and neat flower beds of my own neighborhood. Within the garden were all the essential elements of habitat—cover and nesting places, water for drinking and bathing, and a myriad of food and nectar plants, including flowers, fruit trees, and vegetable patch. All of this on an average residential lot!

Although informal, the garden was neither messy nor neglected. Curving paths led to fragrant stands of flowering bushes or to the benches under the shady grape arbor. In the summer, daisies, black-eyed Susans, zinnias, and hollyhocks swayed together in colorful profusion. Along the fence, behind the vegetable patch, fluffy milkweed, dandelion, and other wild plants drew crowds of pollinators. Like the forest floor, the garden plants grew closely together, yet a kind of relaxed order prevailed among the tangle of trees, flowers, vines, and bushes.

Probably one third of the garden was edible plants—one third ornamentals and another third native trees, shrubs, and flowers—a good mix for habitat. A diversity of plants brings insects. The supply of insects feeds the "beneficials"—the predator insects, the birds, toads, frogs, and lizards. Nectar flowers bring the hummingbirds, bees, butterflies, and other pollinators. Other food plants feed the butterfly caterpillar or provide seeds, berries and nuts for the birds, who will also eat some of the caterpillars. Supporting this whole cycle of life and witnessing its richness and beauty can be a transforming experience and a good path toward finding our way back into nature.

ACKNOWLEDGMENTS

The Wildlife Habitat Garden at the Harvest for the Hungry Garden in Santa Rosa was created in spring 1998, funded by the Sonoma County Community Foundation. Thanks to Lyn Howe's initial vision and dedication, the Habitat Garden has become a beautiful work in progress, bringing together Lyn's experience in creating bird habitat and my passion for butterflies. In the very first summer, the Habitat Garden attracted 14 species of butterflies and many varieties of birds and beneficial insects. Nature responds, even with the smallest effort.

From our experiences and those of other habitat gardeners, we created a manual for our first series of summer workshops on habitat gardening. Revised and expanded, this guide includes Lyn's extensive contributions to the original manual, especially her knowledge of plants and years of experience creating bird habitat.

Mentors Don Mahoney, Barbara Deutsch, and Louise Hallberg guided my habitat gardening journey from the very beginning. Their dedication and love of wildlife continue to inspire me. Butterfly gardeners Karen Tillinghast and Judy Crawford were always willing to share plants and information.

For her wizardry in transforming caterpillar into butterfly, special kudos to book designer Rita Ter Sarkissoff of Spring Hill Press. Many thanks to Jeff Caldwell, George Finger, Judy Brinkerhoff, and Leila Sirk for their edits and support, and my heartfelt gratitude to Terry Byrnes and Judy Adler for their suggestions, encouragement, and dedication to spreading the word.

TABLE OF CONTENTS

HABITAT GARDEN BASICS

*N*ature loves diversity. Imitate nature by planting a wide variety of food and nectar plants that are compatible with our climate.

*H*abitat gardens are natural gardens. They are easy to maintain, conserve water, and do not require fertilizers, pesticides, and herbicides.

*N*ative plants bring in birds, butterflies, and beneficial insects because they have evolved together. They are the plants best adapted to our climate.

*N*atural habitat has a layered look. Trees, shrubs, flowers, grasses, and vines offer food and shelter to many different creatures. So do logs, dead trees, and brush piles.

A general (and flexible) habitat formula: 1/3 natives, 1/3 ornamentals, and 1/3 edible plants (fruit and nut trees, herbs, vegetables, berries).

*A*ll wildlife need water.

*H*abitat gardens are for people, too. Reconnecting with nature, healing a small piece of the earth, and being surprised by the unexpected are just a few of the rewards.

# BUTTERFLY HABITAT

Across a continent of breathtaking diversity we've planted the same two or three dozen plants.

JANET MARINELLI, *Going Native*

Host Plants for Common Butterflies

The following caterpillar host plants will entice some of the most common butterflies in the San Francisco Bay Region to your garden. Most plants in each group can be found in plant nurseries or through seed catalogs. A few of them—plantain, fennel, cheeseweed, Queen Anne's Lace—grow wild in meadows and weedy areas. *See the Appendix for a more complete list of butterflies and caterpillar host plants for this region.*

Host Plants   ## Butterflies

Mallow family
- Checkerbloom
- Lavatera
- Hollyhock
- Cheeseweed

Checkerbloom

West Coast Lady

- Painted Lady
- West Coast Lady
- Common Checkered Skipper
- Gray Hairstreak

Snapdragon family
- Plantain
- Linaria
- Snapdragon
- Monkey Flower
- Owl's Clover

Snapdragon

Buckeye

- Common Buckeye

Fennel

Parsley family
- Fennel*
- Parsley
- Lovage
- Angelica
- Queen Anne's Lace

• Wild Fennel is considered an exotic pest plant.

Anise Swallowtail Caterpillar

- Anise Swallowtail

Milkweed

- Milkweed

Monarch Caterpillar

- Monarch

Willow

- Willows

Tiger Swallowtail

- Western Tiger Swallowtail
- Lorquin's Admiral
- Mourning Cloak

Oak

- Oaks

Spring Azure

- Spring Azure
- California Sister
- Mournful Duskywing

Carex

- Grasses
- Carex

Fiery Skipper

- Grass Skippers
- California Ringlet

3

A Caterpillar is a Butterfly

One of the easiest ways to begin is to plant for butterflies. When you plant for butterflies, remember to plant for the caterpillar, too.

The female butterfly lays her eggs on one or several specific host plants that will provide food for her young. Some host plants are weedy non-native plants—fennel, wild radish, field mustard, cheeseweed— that grow along roadsides, in meadows, and in vacant lots. Native trees and shrubs such as oaks, willows, alders, California lilac, dogwood, and coffeeberry are host plants. So are some wildflowers, grasses, and vines. Many host plants, especially the natives, are not invasive and are easy to grow in almost any kind of landscape.

Contrary to popular opinion, butterfly caterpillars don't chew their way through your garden eating everything in sight. They stay on the host plants, pruning as they eat and grow, giving back frass (caterpillar droppings) as fertilizer. Even though smaller host plants may look ragged, they will come back. As they grow, caterpillars periodically shed their skin, sometimes taking on a whole new look. With their many color combinations and protective disguises, caterpillars are fascinating and comical. Take the bright green caterpillar of the Western Tiger Swallowtail, for example, with its blue spots and large, fake yellow eyes (to scare away predators), or the Anise Swallowtail caterpillar with its orange "horns" that pop out of its head when disturbed.

With a bunch of predators to outlast, not many of those tiny caterpillars make it to the pupal stage, the next step in their life cycle. When they stop eating, caterpillars wander away from the host plant to attach to twigs, dead branches, rocks—even windowsills. Held by a silken thread, the caterpillar rests in the form of a chrysalis for as little as two weeks or, sometimes, as long as two years. Within this form, the structure of the caterpillar is reorganized as it transforms into a creature of flight. Because chrysalids often hide under dead leaves and on twigs and branches, they are sometimes tossed out with the garden trimmings. *That's one reason why butterflies and tidy gardens don't mix. That layer of dead leaves also provides protective mulch for plants in the winter, holds in moisture and offers food and cover for insects (an essential food supply for songbirds and other creatures).*

Emerging from the chrysalis, the butterfly once again faces insects, birds and other predators. For the average butterfly, the spin of the wheel is brief—a mere two weeks. Some species live longer (summer generations of monarchs may live up to eight months), and some hibernate or migrate in the winter. For the lucky butterflies, a stunning feast of colorful, fragrant nectar flowers awaits them. Male and female butterflies mate, and as she feeds, the female butterfly searches for the host plant. Once she's found it, she deposits her eggs and the life cycle begins again. If you plant for butterflies, you will bring in other beneficial insects and birds, which are the predators of insect pests. They'll also eat good bugs and some of the butterfly caterpillars, too. It's all part of the plan: in the food chain, everything is another creature's lunch.

Butterfly Nectar Flowers

Butterflies look for food in sunny, wind-sheltered gardens that offer colorful, fragrant nectar flowers massed together. They like the nectar-rich flowers of the aster family—asters, gloriosa daisy, coreopsis, purple coneflower, marigold, zinnias, sunflowers. Butterflies are also attracted to tightly clustered tubular flowers, such as yarrow, statice, lantana, heliotrope, red valerian, and verbena. These densely packed food sources offer multiple nectar sites in just one spot.

There are many good nectar plants, but some easily fall into the chocolate sundae category. Massed in a sunny garden, buddleia (butterfly bush), *verbena bonariensis,* and tithonia (Mexican sunflower) are guaranteed to bring in any butterfly within striking distance. These fast-food beacons deliver pleasure in many forms—nectar, color, and long-lasting blooms. Native plants, however, are the dependable mainstays of any butterfly habitat. Many of these plants double as caterpillar food plants and excellent nectar sources. Butterflies depend on native wildflowers, shrubs, and trees, such as ceanothus, California buckeye, and dogwood for early spring bloom. Native buckwheats and asters, coyote bush, and goldenrod provide much needed nectar in the fall when other plants are spent.

Like all wildlife, butterflies need a water source. They like to puddle in moist earth where they seek minerals and moisture. Butterflies need wetness, however, more than water. A mud puddle, a shallow saucer filled with wet sand or water and pebbles, or a fine, misting spray on rocks are good watering holes for butterflies.

BUTTERFLY HABITAT BASICS

*M*ass colorful, fragrant, nectar-rich flowers in a sunny, sheltered area. Choose plants that bloom in different seasons.

· *P*lace caterpillar food plants near nectar plants.

· *B*e less eager to prune and rake. Check for chrysalids and butterfly eggs hidden in the trimmings.

*L*arge sun-baked rocks make good perching sites. A mud puddle or shallow saucer of water provides moisture and minerals.

· *A*void pesticides. Butterflies are extremely sensitive to chemicals. Especially avoid using the pesticide alternative Bt (Bacillus thuringiensis) in your butterfly garden. It is fatal to caterpillars.

7

Good Butterfly Plants

The following list includes some of the best butterfly food and nectar plants for the San Francisco Bay Region, natives and non-natives, covering spring through fall seasons. They are low water-use plants and sun-lovers unless otherwise noted.

Note that most butterfly habitat plants are also attractive to birds and insects.

Key to Symbols   Birds   Hummingbirds   Insects

Trees

California Buckeye • *Aesculus californica (native)*
Early spring blooms provide a long supply of nectar; a caterpillar food plant for the Spring Azure. Can be pruned to grow as a large shrub. Deciduous; drops leaves early.

Oak • *Quercus spp. (native)*
Caterpillar food plant for Mournful Duskywing, California Hairstreak, California Sister, Spring Azure. The mistletoe that grows in some oaks is caterpillar food for the Great Purple Hairstreak. Evergreen varieties are more useful as habitat plants.

Strawberry Tree • *Arbutus unedo*

Clusters of white flowers and red fruit on this beautiful evergreen tree appear summer through fall. Good nectar plant. *A. unedo* 'Compacta' is a smaller version.

Willow • *Salix (native & non-native species)*

Caterpillar food plant for Lorquin's Admiral, Mourning Cloak, and Western Tiger Swallowtail. Early bloomers; most willows need summer water and grow best near streams or ponds. The flexible, fresh branches provide good material for small trellises. Deciduous.

Shrubs

Butterfly Bush • *Buddleia davidii*

Highly desirable plant with fragrant blooms in shades of lilac, purple, yellow. Large deciduous shrub to 15 ft.; also a smaller variety. Blooms all summer.

California Coffeeberry • *Rhamnus californica (native)*

This attractive evergreen shrub (3–14 ft.) is a caterpillar food plant for the Gray Hairstreak and Pale Swallowtail; small greenish flowers provide nectar in spring.

9

California Lilac • *Ceanothus (many native species)*
Many varieties available from large shrubs to low ground covers. Its fragrant early blooms in shades of blue and purple provide a good nectar source in spring. Caterpillar food plant for Spring Azure, California Tortoiseshell, California Hairstreak, Hedgerow Hairstreak. Good for hot, dry areas (coastal varieties also available).

Chaste Tree • *Vitex agnus-castus*
Beautiful nectar-rich spikes, attractive foliage and long bloom period. A daintier version of the buddleia. Makes good screen/hedge; bushy to 15 ft. Will tolerate partial shade; deer avoid it. Deciduous.

Creambush • *Holodiscus discolor (native)*
A deciduous shrub (3-6 ft.) with fragrant and showy creamy white sprays. It likes partial shade and tolerates heat; better with some summer water. Caterpillar food plant for Spring Azure, Pale Swallowtail, Lorquin's Admiral.

Flowering Currants • *Ribes* spp. *(native)*
Excellent nectar plants. A larval plant for the Tailed Copper butterfly.

Tree Mallow • *Lavatera assurgentiflora (native)*
Also non-native species
Fast-growing, long blooming and airy shrub with showy pink flowers. Good nectar plant and caterpillar food plant for West Coast Lady, Painted Lady, Common Checkered Skipper, Gray Hairstreak. Evergreen.

Perennials • Annuals

Asters • *(many species; perennials)*

All asters are good nectar plants. Michaelmas Daisy (aster hybrid), *A. frikarti,* and *A. nova-belgii* are especially good for fall bloom.

California Aster • *Aster chilensis (native perennial)*

Excellent nectar plant that blooms in the fall. Shrubby to 2 ft. tall with lavender flowers; spreads through rhizomes. May stay green through winter. Caterpillar food plant for Northern Checkerspot and Field Crescent.

Bee Plant • *Scrophularia californica (native perennial)*

Attractive foliage on tall plant (3–6 ft.) Tiny dark red flowers look like miniature orchids; provide nectar over long period for pollinators. Caterpillar food plant for Chalcedon Checkerspot.

Wild Buckwheat • *Eriogonum* spp. *(native perennials)*

Caterpillar food plant for Acmon Blue, Green Hairstreak, Purplish Copper, Gorgon Copper. Buckwheats, including *E. latifolium, E. nudum,* and *E. umbellatum* (sulfur buckwheat), are exceptional nectar sources for butterflies in spring.

Bur Marigold • *Bidens laevis (native perennial)*

An exceptional nectar plant for an attractive border along paths, flower beds, or near ponds. Bright yellow flowers from spring through fall.

11

Checkerbloom • *Sildalcea malvaeflora*
(native perennial)

Low-growing with soft pink blooms. Sildalcea is a caterpillar food and nectar plant for West Coast Lady, Painted Lady, Common Checkered Skipper, Gray Hairstreak. Easy to grow in pots.

Common Coyote Mint • *Monardella villosa*
(native perennial)

Pinkish-lavender blooms on low-growing evergreen plant that forms mats. Excellent nectar plant for edges of flowerbeds, along walkways; summer bloom. Prefers dry conditions.

Goldenrod • *Solidago* spp.
(native & non-native perennials)

Tall, golden plumes produce abundant nectar in late summer and fall. Often mistaken for a plant that causes allergic reactions.

Hollyhock • *Alcea rosa (generally treated as annual)*

Nectar plant and caterpillar food plant for West Coast Lady, Painted Lady, Common Checkered Skipper. Many colors; single flower varieties best.

Mexican Sunflower • *Tithonia rotundifolia*
(annual)

Exceptional nectar plant with profuse, showy orange flowers; especially attractive to Monarchs. Bushy to 3 ft. with lots of sun and heat.

Milkweed • *Asclepias* spp. *(native & non-native)*

Flower clusters range from yellow-orange to creamy white; showy, unusual seed pods. All species are caterpillar food plants (they also provide nectar) for the Monarch. Semi-dry conditions; water in growth stage.

- *A. curassavica:* frost-tender; easy to grow in pots
- *A. eriocarpa (native):* hardy perennial; can tolerate dry conditions
- *A. incarnata (eastern U.S. native):* hardy, but likes moist conditions
- *A. fascicularis (native):* hardy perennial; blooms June-September
- *A. speciosa (native):* hardy perennial; fragrant flowers; blooms June-August

Parsley Family: Lovage • Angelica • Parsley • Cow Parsnip

Flat, umbrella-shaped flower heads. Caterpillar food plants for Anise Swallowtail.

Pincushion Flower • *Scabiosa* spp.
(annuals & perennials)

Attractive lavender, pink, white or dark maroon long blooming nectar flowers on tall stems. Reseeds.

Purple Coneflower • *Echinacea purpurea (perennial)*

Deep pink flowers have dark cone-shaped center. Excellent nectar plant.

Red Valerian • *Centranthus ruber (perennial)*
Rosy flower clusters on spreading stems.
Hardy; takes hot, dry spots. Blooms spring
through fall. Good nectar plant.

Sage • *Salvia* spp.
(many native & non-native perennials)
Fragrant sages are wonderful habitat plants.
Airy, soft blue Bog Sage *(S. uliginosa)* likes wet
feet and is excellent for clay soils; *S. Indigo
Spires, S. pitcherii, S. guaranitica,* and *S. sclarea*
are just a few butterfly favorites.

Seaside Daisy (Beach Aster) • *Erigeron glaucus
(native perennial)*
This low-growing, hardy native blooms up to
six months. Can stand severe winter frosts.

Verbena bonariensis • *(perennials)*
A top nectar plant; tall and airy with clusters
of purple-pink flowers. Mass for best effect.
Other verbenas—*V. rigida, V. canadensis,
V. gooddingi*—are also good nectar plants.

Yarrow • *Achillea millefolium (native perennial)*
Summer-blooming white flower with fern-like
foliage provides good nectar source; cultivars
come in many colors.

14

Zinnia spp. • *(annual)*
Heirloom varieties better; effective nectar
source when massed. Long summer/fall
bloom. Many rich colors.

Vines

Dutchman's Pipe • *Aristolochia californica*
(native perennial)
A deciduous, woody vine with large heart-
shaped leaves and distinctive pipe-shaped
flowers. A slow grower, it can be difficult to
get started; requires shade for roots, moisture,
and a trellis or shrub to climb on. Only caterpillar food plant for the Pipevine Swallowtail.
Avoid *A. elegans,* which is fatal to Pipevine
Swallowtail larvae.

Hops • *Humulus lupulus (perennial)*
Rapidly growing deciduous vine. Caterpillar
food plant for Red Admiral and Satyr
Anglewing, two butterflies that prefer riparian
habitat.

15

Grasses • Ground Covers

The grass Skippers and the California Ringlet use grasses as caterpillar food plants. Purple Needle Grass and Bluegrass (Poa) are food plants for the California Ringlet. The skippers in this region use various lawn grasses and native bunchgrasses—Rye Grass, Red Fescue, Tufted Hair Grass, Carex. Try beautiful native bunch-grasses for gardens, meadows, lawns, and for erosion control on steep banks. Berkeley sedge *(Carex tumicola),* a Bay Area native, stays green year-round with minimal water and takes sun or shade. Deergrass *(Muhlenbergia rigens),* a large native bunchgrass with tall panicles 3-feet high, makes a beautiful specimen plant or use for hedges, edging, or erosion control.

Myoporum parvifolium 'Putah Creek'
A dense, evergreen groundcover with white summer flowers followed by purple berries that is hardy and fast-growing. Water to establish; looks better with some summer water. A good butterfly nectar plant.

Lippia repens
Forms a sturdy flat mat that goes dormant in the winter. The small rose flowers that bloom from spring to fall are a favorite nectar plant of the grass Skippers and other butterflies.

Lavatera

Aster

Verbena

Hops

Blue Oat Grass, Seaside Daisy, Buckwheat

17

BIRD HABITAT

Whatever special nests we make—leaves, moss or tents or piled stone—we all dwell in a house of one room.

JOHN MUIR

Birds Take the Big Roles

*From hummingbirds to hawks, from finches to quail, birds
take the big roles on the habitat stage as they soar, sing,
and dazzle. Bluebirds, flycatchers, and swallows scoop the
air for bugs. Hummingbirds announce their arrival with
loud wing buzzes as they fight for territory or skyrocket
through the air in flashy mating flights.*

Each level of cover—trees, shrubs, grasses, and ground
cover—provides shelter, foraging, and nesting sites
for different species of birds. Quail, towhees, and juncos
prefer the underbrush where they feed on tender shoots,
buds, and seeds. In the shrubbery, bushtits climb through
the branches looking for insects, while the nuthatches
stay high in the trees. A dead tree is home to woodpeckers, wrens, bluebirds, and tree swallows, but it becomes
hummingbird heaven with honeysuckle or trumpet vine
twining around it. Brush piles, even small ones, make
great bird cover. If your plant shelters also produce nuts,
fruit or berries, more birds will visit. Berry-producing
native plants such as blue elderberry, hollyleaf cherry,
toyon, and California coffeeberry are better choices for
the garden than non-native pyracantha or invasive privet
and cotoneaster.

To keep birds as residents, food sources need to be
available throughout the seasons. A diversity of flowers,
trees, and shrubs that bloom at different times offer a
constant source of nectar, insects, seeds, and berries. The
more you have, the more species of birds you will attract.
Hummingbirds, for example, nest as early as December
and require rich sources of nectar and protein (insects).
Plant as many natives as possible. Birds will choose the
native plants they evolved with first: these are the plants

that provide them with all of their nutritional needs. One of the best year-round native shrubs is coyote bush *(Baccharis pilularis)*. Its late blooming flowers attract many insects in the autumn. Some birds, such as the wrentit and white-crowned sparrow, use coyote bush for all their needs—perching, eating, nesting, and breeding.

Hummingbird Havens

As part of its mating ritual, a male hummingbird skyrockets straight up into the sky, briefly disappears, then suddenly plunges downward in a noisy kamikaze dive. The first time I witnessed this performance, I was more impressed, I guarantee, than the lady friend. These tiny birds are anything but timid, as any hummingbird gardener knows. Both males and females aggressively defend their territory from larger birds, and especially from other hummers. Fierce competitiveness is not surprising given the critical importance of their food source. To support a very fast metabolism and those high-speed chases, hummers need a constant source of nutrients. With their long tongues, they sip sucrose in the form of nectar from flowers, scooping up small insects as they feed or catching them on the fly (yet another reason not to use pesticides—they not only contaminate flowers, but also kill the insects birds feed on.)

Anna's hummingbird, our year-round resident, is the one you are most likely to see in your garden. The male is dark green with a red head and throat. Though the female may wear a few iridescent feathers on her throat, she is far less showy. Three migrants—the black-chinned hummingbird, the rufous hummingbird, and Allen's hummingbird—visit the Bay Region from early spring through summer. Many of our native trees and shrubs—

manzanita, California lilac, California buckeye, pink flowering currant—bloom just in time for their arrival.

So do coral bells, foxgloves, monkey flowers, and columbine, each of them bearing clusters of tubular flowers on tall stems or spikes. If these tubular flowers happen to be red, so much the better. It's not that hummers won't stop at flowers of other colors, it's just that red monkey flowers or red penstemons or the bright orange spikes of the red-hot poker plant catch their attention more quickly.

It's a good idea to offer nectar sources in all seasons, of course. Fall and winter generally pose the most problems. Once again, the natives come through. Bright, orange-flowered California fuchsias, a nectar-rich ground cover for dry, sunny places, bloom late summer into fall. The bright pink clusters of two native flowering currants offer rich sources of nectar when not much else is blooming: *Ribes sanguineum* flowers as early as January and likes dry, sunny places; *Ribes malvaceum*, which needs some water, may be blooming through winter into March. Salvias are "must-haves" in a hummingbird habitat. Their spicy fragrance attracts many pollinators, though hummingbirds are attracted to the shape of the flowers rather than the scent. They come in many colors, many delightful forms. Most of them like sun and dry conditions.

All birds, including hummers, need water. Water in a birdbath, saucer or pond, trickling over rocks, misting and gurgling from a fountain offers a place for birds (and other wildlife) to splash or take a quick drink. The smallest offering—a large rock with a depression deep enough to hold water—will not go unnoticed.

BIRD HABITAT BASICS

*P*lant many different kinds of flowers, trees, and shrubs (especially natives) that bloom in different seasons.

*I*n the fall, don't deadhead your flowers. Let them go to seed to provide food for finches, juncos, and other seedeaters.

*P*lace bird baths near shrubs and trees to provide cover, especially from cats, but also far enough away to prevent attacks from cats hiding in the shrubbery. Though birds have many predators, it is estimated that domestic cats kill from 2 to 4 million songbirds daily in the U.S. Whenever possible, keep them out of habitat areas, especially during nesting season.

*A*void cutting trees or pruning shrubs during nesting season, which usually lasts from late spring to August.

*I*f you use hummingbird feeders, make sure you wash them thoroughly at each refill. If you are on vacation and can't keep them clean, it's better to take them down rather than risk infecting your local hummers.

*M*ost important of all, don't use insecticides and other poisons. Make your garden a safe sanctuary for yourself and local wildlife.

23

Good Plants for Bird Habitat

Any tree, shrub, or flower that is good habitat for insects will provide food for 90 to 95% of the songbird species. Their young cannot mature without a diet of insects, and many adults are also dependent on insects for food. Flowering plants not only supply nectar for birds such as orioles and hummingbirds, but also attract many kinds of insects, an additional food source. The plants listed below are low-water use plants, unless otherwise noted, and suitable for San Francisco Bay Area gardens. Note that many bird habitat plants are also attractive to butterflies and other insects.

Note: In addition to the birds listed for specific plants, many other species of birds may also use the plant.

Key to Symbols
Hummingbird Butterflies Insects

Trees

California Bay Laurel • *Umbellularia californica*
(native)
Small, fragrant flowers bloom from December to May, which attract the insectivores. Warblers, towhees, chickadees forage in leaf litter for insects. Aromatic leaves help deter feather mites. Evergreen.

California Buckeye • *Aesculus californica (native)*

Early summer blooms provide nectar supply for several months. Attractive to hummingbirds, orioles, black-headed grosbeaks, migrating warblers. Deciduous.

Oak • *Quercus (many native species)*

Best plant for all around bird use. Acorns for woodpeckers, ducks, jays; insects available all year. Oaks provide nest sites for owls, hawks, and small cavity nesters (titmouse, wren, woodpecker, nuthatch). The berries of the mistletoe that grow in oaks feed cedar waxwings, orioles, western bluebirds. Leaf litter offers excellent foraging sites for the towhee, thrush, and quail. Evergreen varieties best for habitat.

Toyon (Christmas Berry) • *Heteromeles arbutifolia (native)*

Bright red berry clusters through autumn and winter provide food for many birds, such as hermit and Swainson's thrush, purple finches, cedar waxwings, mockingbirds. Evergreen.

Western Chokeberry • *Prunus virginiana demissa (native)*

One of the most valuable food plants, cover, and nesting sites for birds. Ivory plumes bring in an early insect supply; garnet berries in summer. Very rapid growth; needs pruning. Deciduous.

Willow • *Salix (native species)*

Early blooms attract insects. Nesting sites and unripe capsules for sparrows, finches, warblers, thrushes. Deciduous. Most willows need summer water.

25

Shrubs

Blue Elderberry • *Sambucus mexicana (native)*
The Blue Elderberry is the favorite of many bird species. Its beautiful creamy flowers attract insects and the berries are loved by tanagers, grosbeaks, and many others. Large deciduous shrub. Will grow back vigorously when cut back in winter.

California Coffeeberry • *Rhamnus californica (native)*
A handsome, fast-growing evergreen shrub that takes sun or part shade. Berries turn black in the fall attracting many species, including the band-tailed pigeon.

California Lilac • *Ceanothus (many native species)*
Attractive, popular native forms low ground cover or large shrub. Fragrant, early bloom in shades of blue. Insects for tanagers, shrikes, and others. Nectar for hummingbirds; seed for bushtits, finches. Mostly evergreen.

Coyote Bush • *Baccharis pilularis; B. 'Twin Peaks' (native)*
Mid-fall bloom attracts more than 450 species of insects, also warblers. Seed available for bushtits, white-crowned sparrows, and others. Good shelter and nest site. Evergreen.

Flowering Currants • *Ribes malvaceum, R. sanguineum (other native species)*

Plant *R. sanguineum* for crimson-pink pendants in January and *R. malvaceum* for bright rose flowers October-March. Excellent sources of nectar for hummingbirds. Deciduous.

Dogwood • *Cornus* spp. *(native species)*

Provides nest sites, fruit, and insects for as many as 20 bird species, including Bullock's oriole, thrashers, grosbeaks, tanagers, towhees, and thrush. Of the six California natives, brown dogwood *(C. glabrata)* is particularly good for attracting birds. It's a beautiful ornamental shrub with arching branches, reddish twigs, and small, creamy white flowers. Easily shaped with careful pruning. Deciduous; better with some shade.

Island Bush Snapdragon • *Galvezia speciosa (native)*

A beautiful, drought-tolerant evergreen shrub that blooms most of the year with bright red flowers that look like snapdragons. Frost-tender; mulch well. Hummingbirds love it.

Manzanita • *Arctostaphylos (many native species)*

Manzanitas vary in size from large trees to low mounding shrubs. Attractive form with wine-red trunks. Pink bell-shaped flowers offer an early nectar source for insects. Anna's hummingbirds will stay year-round for the nectar and insect protein it provides. Evergreen.

27

Wax Myrtle • *Myrica californica (native)*
An evergreen shrub with catkin flowers, small purple-brown fruits, and glossy leaves that are fragrant when crushed. Provides shade and moisture. Flickers, thrush, warblers are particularly fond of it.

Perennials • Annuals

Many flowering perennials and annuals provide some source of food for birds. Blooms provide nectar and attract insects. A variety of seedeaters, such as titmouse, finch, and grosbeak, feed on the seed in the fall.

Bee Balm • *Monarda didyma (perennial & annual)*
A favorite of hummingbirds, this bushy plant blooms in the fall in shades of red and lavender.

California Fuchsia • *Epilobium (Zauschneria)* spp.
(native perennials)
The scarlet flowers that bloom in the fall are loved by hummingbirds. *Zauschneria* makes an attractive ground cover in full sun and is good for banks and dry areas.

Columbine • *Aquilegia formosa*
(native & non-native perennials)
The native species, *A. formosa*, and *A. eximia*, are preferred by hummingbirds. Bright red flowers with yellow stamens bloom May until late summer. Prefers some shade and moisture.

Evening Primrose • *Oenothera hookeri*
(native biennial)
Tall (to 14 ft.) with large, sunny yellow flowers,
this plant is a valuable asset for bird habitat.
The seedpods are relished by finches and
juncos. It attracts insects for fall migrating
warblers and finches. Reseeds readily. ●

Mexican Sunflower • *Tithonia rotundifolia (annual)*
The bright orange 3-inch flowers offer seed
for juncos, finches, and grosbeaks. It grows
vigorously with sun and heat.

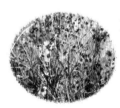

Penstemon spp. • *(native & non-native perennials)*
Penstemons are hardy and beautiful nectar
plants that come in many colors and varieties.
Hummingbirds are especially fond of Firebird
Penstemon and Scarlet Bugler Penstemon *(P.
centranthifolius)*.

Plains Coreopsis • *Coreopsis tinctoria (annual)*
Hardy upright plant with airy look and
profuse yellow flowers with maroon centers.
Large quantities of seed in the fall for finches,
juncos, sparrows, titmouse.

Rosemary • *Rosmarinus officinalis*
(evergreen herb, shrub)
Profuse blue flowers in early spring attract
insects, especially pollinators; nectar for
hummingbirds; good cover for ground birds.

Sage • *Salvia (many native & non-native species)*

All sages attract hummingbirds, goldfinches, and other seedeaters, pollinating insects, and butterflies. They provide winter cover for sparrows and towhees. Most salvias like sun.

NATIVE PERENNIALS

• *S. clevelandii.* Hardy, small shrub with gray-green foliage and spires of fragrant blue flowers. Prefers dry sunny conditions.

• *S. leucophylla.* Low-spreading shrub with white, fuzzy leaves and pink flower clusters. Likes it dry and sunny.

• *S. sononomensis.* Creeping ground cover with lavender flowers; dry and sunny conditions.

• *S. spathacea.* Whorls of magenta bloom with fragrant leaves. Prefers some shade.

NON-NATIVE ANNUAL & PERENNIAL SAGES

• *S. coccinea* (Red Sage). Annual; short with attractive red flowers.

• *S. elegans* (Pineapple Sage). Red flowers in late fall; a tender perennial and a hummingbird favorite.

• *S. involucrata.* Beet-colored tender perennial that blooms late summer (to 5 ft.).

• *S. leucantha* (Mexican Sage). Bushy perennial with long lavender spikes and a long bloom period (to 4 ft.).

• *S. uliginosa* (Bog Sage). Airy perennial with soft blue spikes; good choice for clay soils (to 5 ft.).

Torch Lily (Hot Poker Plant) • *Kniphofia uvaria*
(perennial)
Tall, torch shaped spikes with tubular orange/
yellow flowers densely packed at the tips. A
favorite nectar source for orioles and hummingbirds.

Wild Rose • *Rosa californica (native perennial)*
Wild rose thickets form excellent sites for
ground-nesters (quail and towhees). Great
forage sites and cover for all birds. Rose hips
for goldfinches and pine siskins; single, deep-
pink fragrant flowers.

Vines

Chaparral Clematis • *Clematis lasiantha (native)*
Large fluffy seed heads with 2-inch creamy
white flowers. Climbs through shrubs and
trees to 15–18 ft.

Honeysuckle • *Lonicera* spp.
(native & non-native perennials)
L. hispidula has pink flowers and scarlet
berries; *L. ciliosa* (orange honeysuckle),
orange-red berries; *L. involucrata* (black
twinberry), shiny black berries (prefers some
shade and regular moisture). Attractive to
hummingbirds and finches. Evergreen.

Western Virgin's Bower • *Clematis ligusticifolia (native)*

A fast growing vine with fragrant white flowers and showy seedpods. Good cover and seed.

Wild Grape • *Vitis californica (native)*

The berries of this deciduous vine attract mockingbirds, waxwings, thrush, and many other species. The variety 'Roger's Red' turns a beautiful shade in the fall. Caterpillar food plant for sphinx moth.

California Wildflowers

Wildflowers—Tidy Tips, Clarkia, Gilia, Tarweed, Lupine, Blue Flax, Five Spot, Baby Blue Eyes, California Poppy, Tansy-Leaf Phacelia, Goldfields, Miners Lettuce—provide seed and insect supply for birds.

# HABITAT
FOR
BENEFICIAL INSECTS

... *If plants, including many food and forage crops, as well as natural floras, must have insects to exist, then human beings must have insects to exist.*

E. O. WILSON, *The Forgotten Pollinators*

FRIENDLY INSECT
PREDATORS & POLLINATORS

Wren
> Did you know that a wren can consume more than 500 insect eggs, beetles, and grubs in one afternoon?

Garden Spiders
> Predators of moths, crickets, grasshoppers, and many other insects

Wasps
> Pollinators (also parasitic insects)

Dragonfly
> Eats flies and mosquitoes; needs a water garden, pond, or stream

Damselfly
> Eats many insects, including aphids; needs water garden, pond, or stream

Lacewing
> Larvae feed on aphids and other insects

Soldier Beetle
> Predator of cucumber beetles, grasshopper eggs, aphids, caterpillars

Ground Beetle
> Eats snails, slugs, and gypsy moth larvae

Ladybug
> Predator of aphids and other pests

Hummingbird
> Pollinator that also feeds on small insects

Honeybee
> Pollinator; produces honey, pollen, and beeswax

Bumblebee
> Pollinator of potatoes, tomatoes, and other crops

Solitary Native Bees
> Specialized pollinators of food plants and wildflowers

Hover Fly & Tachinid Fly
> Excellent pollinators; their young consume aphids

A LITTLE FRIENDLY ADVICE

Avoid pesticides.

If you spray, you may kill a few of the "pests," but you will certainly kill off the larger and more susceptible beneficial insects as well. Then you risk an outbreak of many pests, who no longer have predators to keep them in check.

Grow a diversity of plants.

By growing many different kinds of plants that bloom in all seasons, you create an attractive environment for the insects that predator bugs eat.

Consider a policy of coexistence with honeybees.

Unless you are allergic to their sting, tolerate honeybees in your habitat. Honeybees do not prey on humans. When a honeybee stings, it's a desperate action.

Insects are the Balance

Insects keep the garden in balance by pollinating plants, keeping each other's numbers in check, and providing food for birds and other predators. When you clean up leaves and brush to discourage insects, you are also cleaning up the food supply of 90 percent of the songbirds. And most species hawk for insects to provide protein for their young.

Native plant hedgerows—the ideal windbreak or screen for front yards, backyards, orchards and vineyards—are the perfect habitat for beneficial insects. A native plant row increases biodiversity and offers shelter, nesting sites, and food sources (insects, berries, nectar) for birds and other wildlife. By planting a diverse group of natives, the hedgerow will be in bloom year-round to attract tiny parasitic wasps, hover flies, and tachinid flies, minute pirate bugs, lady beetles, assassin bugs, and other beneficial species. These scary-sounding bugs attack the eggs and larvae of potential insect pests, such as aphids, scales, mealybugs, stinkbugs, squash bugs, thrips, and spider mites. California lilac, manzanita, toyon, blue elderberry, coffeeberry, coyote bush, holly-leaf cherry, quailbush, California wild rose, California buckwheat, and Mexican sage are top hedgerow choices.

Some insect predators are also pollinators looking for tasty food plants that not only supply other insects but also provide pollen and nectar. Beneficial flies and tiny parasitic wasps, for example, are pollinators that do not sting or bite. Their larvae generally feed on host insects such as sawflies, borers, or cabbageworms. Plant native wildflowers (tidytips, baby blue eyes, tansy-leaf phacelia), sweet alyssum, goldenrod, and the umbellifers (carrots, fennel, parsley, dill, angelica, Queen Anne's lace, lovage, bishop flower) near the vegetable garden, in flowerbeds and planter boxes. Members of the sunflower family— cosmos, dandelion, yarrow, feverfew, Gloriosa daisy, zinnias—are also highly favored food plants.

Attract the Perfect Urban Pollinator

A more efficient pollinator than the honeybee, the orchard mason bee is non-aggressive and is especially useful for early blooming plants, such as fruit and nut trees (the bees usually die by early June). The mason bee lays its eggs in numerous unused beetle holes, rather than in hives. They use mud or clay to build their nests. To encourage a large pollinating population of mason bees in your garden or orchard, provide untreated blocks of wood with 5/16" holes (recommended depth is 6 inches) on 3/4" centers.

Tune in to the Ground Level Action

Compost and rock piles, a board on the ground, or an old log makes a home for "beneficials" such as lady-bugs, ground beetles, tiger beetles, rove beetles, soldier bugs, and assassin bugs. Aphids are the favorite feasts of ladybugs, and fast-moving rove beetles are beneficial decomposers in the garden ecosystem. Ground beetles hunt for snails and slugs at night and soldier bugs eat aphids, beetle larvae, and many other insects, including some of the beneficials. Keep a magnifying glass and a guide handy to identify all the good guys in your garden.

Dragonfly Ponds

Perched on sun-warmed boulders in the middle of slow-moving streams or stretched out on the grassy banks of garden ponds, I've spent many dreamy hours watching bronze-winged dragonflies go by. These fascinating and aggressive insect predators have been with us since prehistoric times. A water source in your garden may entice them to drop by, but a marshy pond is true dragonfly habitat.

Though we know them as acrobatic flyers, dragonflies actually live underwater much longer than they breathe air. Hiding out in pond debris and underwater vegetation, dragonfly nymphs prey on mosquito  larvae, aquatic insects, tadpoles, and even tiny fish. They may spend only a winter underwater or as long as two or more years.

After the nymph emerges to shed its skin above water, it may fly for only a few weeks, feeding on mosquitoes and other small insects. Adults need plants above the water line to perch on, and the nymphs need emergent vegetation to crawl up on when they leave the water.

Once in the air, dragonflies are attracted to large, sunny ponds. A deep pond (over 18 inches in depth) protects the nymphs and other pond wildlife from the nocturnal excursions of raccoons. Ideally, a wildlife pond should contain both shallow and deep areas, both steep and sloping sides. Fill the pond with native plants such as mare's tail, horse-tail, blue flag iris, water alyssum, watercress, parrot's feather, and creeping water primrose. Anchor them in pots if the bottom is covered with plastic. Think twice before filling your pond with fish. All fish, including mosquito fish, eat frog and dragonfly eggs. Attract dragonflies and the smaller damselflies, frogs, and toads to your pond, and they will happily perform mosquito patrol.

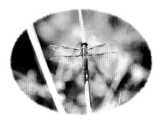

They won't be the only ones enjoying the pond, however. Many species of birds will use the pond for bathing and drinking. Nocturnal animals—fox, skunk, raccoon, opossum, and deer—if they are in your area, may stop for a quick sip. Butterflies and hummingbirds will show up too, especially if you include cardinal flowers among your pond plants. Humans may also be observed playing in their endlessly changing, always relaxing, and frequently magical ponds.

Bugs are Messengers

Living with insects and developing a trust in nature is the path to seeing the garden as refuge, rather than battleground.

Bob Cannard, renowned organic grower in Sonoma County, is an advocate of sustainable agriculture. He has taught and practiced restorative gardening for many years. "Don't take adversity into the garden," Bob tells gardeners, "it's not a war zone out there. Bugs are messengers."

Let's say you find cucumber beetles on your zucchini plants. If they're only eating the oldest leaves and a small number of them, it's to be expected. Eating the oldest parts of the plants is their job. If they are swarming all over the plants, that is a message that the plants are unhealthy. These are not plants you want to feed yourself or your family. If we really pay attention to all of our plants, if we observe them and spend time with them, they can tell us a lot. Is this plant happy in the shade? Are there enough nutrients in the soil? Too much water? Not enough?

What makes a plant healthy and less attractive to insects? Bob Cannard lists four primary food groups essential for healthy plants:

1. Minerals
   Rocks are a vital source of various minerals. Rock dust and oyster shell are excellent sources of minerals for the garden.

2. Good digestion in the soil
   Bacteria and fungi, important ingredients for healthy soil, are present when the soil has an earthy, sweet smell.

3. Sunlight
   The correct amount for the plant and for the season.

4. Air
   Water (liquid air) and carbon (old air from thoroughly digested compost)

By adding minerals and compost to the soil, growing cover crops to ensure adequate carbon, and planting in appropriate seasons, you give your plants a healthy start. Don't forget to use your senses: smell the soil, look at the plants, touch them. That is a better use of our energy than search and destroy missions.

Bob Cannard's Homemade Soil Inoculant

Take a handful of rich, sweet-smelling compost (a small handful from the forest if you hike) or earthworm castings or rabbit manure. Mix with water and (1) milk or juice or (2) a broth (room temperature) made from boiling kitchen scraps or green weeds. Let sit overnight. Put in watering can and sprinkle in garden. Apply regularly until soil smells sweet and clean.

Ladybug eating
aphids

Goldenrod

Comfrey

Exuvia: shed skin of
dragonfly nymph

Blue Flag Iris/
Pickerel Weed

Anise Hyssop

44

GETTING STARTED

> *G*arden **with** *Mother Nature, not against her.*
>
> ANDY WASOWSKI, *The Landscaping Revolution*

Some Habitat Heroes

Native Oaks
According to the California Oak Foundation, 331 wildlife species—birds, mammals, amphibians, and reptiles—use oak woodlands for food, cover, and reproduction. Over 5,000 species of insects, including 7 butterfly species, are also part of this extensive web of life.

Blue Elderberry
This multipurpose plant provides nectar for pollinators, berries for many species of birds, and food for beetles and other insects. It also serves as a beautiful garden plant for hedge, screen, or wind.

Sunflower Family
All members of the sunflower family are excellent habitat plants for nectar and seed. These sun-lovers work in almost any soil, require little water, and just keep on blooming.

Native Buckwheat • *Eriogonum species*
A caterpillar food plant and nectar plant for butterflies, native buckwheats offer seeds, cover, and nectar for many kinds of beneficial insects.

Evening Primrose • *Oenothera hookeri*

The tall, bright yellow evening primrose is both native medicinal herb and daily bird feeder. Each day the seedpods open just far enough to offer one seed. In this way, they provide birds with a continuous supply of seed over a very long period of time. Bees and other pollinators drink nectar from this stunning flower for the back of a sunny and dry border.

Lavender

Culinary & Medicinal Herbs

Culinary herbs such as thyme, rosemary, and dill attract beneficial insects and provide seed for birds. Some plants—tansy, mint, oregano, sage—repel insects, which make them good companions to vulnerable plants. Medicinal herbs are ancient plants that heal the garden, body, and spirit. Bee balm (hummingbirds love it!), lavender, mullein, borage, and calendula (pot marigold), to name just a few, are nectar-rich companions for flowers and food plants.

SOME FIRST STEPS

Just in case you are feeling a bit overwhelmed, remember that you have already started. Which of the habitat essentials—food, water, and nesting sites—are you providing right now? What are you already attracting to your garden, and in what direction would you like to go next? Here are a few ideas.

*T*hink of your landscape as a living component of your life. Allow at least a small part of it to go wild.

*A*dd one or two native plants to the garden in the fall.

*G*row some edibles you would enjoy—vegetables, herbs, fruit trees, or berries.

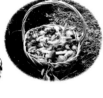

*I*f you like roses, consider fragrant, hardy, old-fashioned climbing roses and native roses. They are more disease resistant and nectar-rich than hybrids.

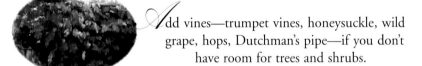

*A*dd vines—trumpet vines, honeysuckle, wild grape, hops, Dutchman's pipe—if you don't have room for trees and shrubs.

*G*row a good compost pile for worms and nutrients for your soil or hide small compost piles of leaves and cuttings throughout the garden.

*K*eep mulch under flowers and shrubs. Use dead leaves, grass clippings, and plant trimmings to enrich your soil, keep in moisture, and to attract beneficial insects, lizards, toads, and frogs. Birds, too, will use these offerings as nesting materials.

GROWING NATIVES

Native plants and native birds, bugs, butterflies, and other wildlife have evolved together. When you plant natives, you're not just adding different plants; you are growing a community. Natives are the plants that are best adapted to our climate. They do not need fertilizers, heavy pruning, or special care. Here are a few basic guidelines.

🐦 *Autumn is the ideal time to plant natives.*

By taking advantage of winter rains, you will encourage long roots for the dry months ahead. Once they are planted, natives will need some water in between rains. A rule of thumb for drought tolerant natives is to water once a week for inland regions and every two weeks for coastal areas until they get established, generally through the first dry season. After that, occasional deep watering during the second year is also advised. Native plants in containers need regular watering. Generally, people make two common mistakes with natives. They water too much, or at the beginning, too little. Until they are established, be careful to not let them dry out. Generally, natives need good drainage.

🐦 *Natives have complex root relationships that keep them healthy, so planting them together, separate from the other plants in the garden, is a good idea.*

If you mix natives with other plants in your garden, be sure they all have the same requirements for sun, shade, soil, and water. (Plants from other Mediterranean climate regions are generally compatible with natives.) Make the planting holes at least twice as wide as the container. Plant high for good drainage, and keep the plant's crown free from mulch or excess soil. Some native perennials die back to the ground in the fall and come back again in the spring; others remain green throughout winter.

🐦 *Find out what native plants grow best in your microclimate.*

Nearby open space and parks with natural plant communities offer clues for what grows best in your area. Native plant nurseries are good resources for information and advice. Try to find out where a native plant naturally grows, what it needs, and how it would fit in your garden.

Final Thoughts

See your piece of land as a part of a larger plant and animal community, maintain any natural vegetation and use natural communities as inspiration for backyard landscape.

JUDITH LARNER LOWRY, *Gardening with a Wild Heart*

It's no secret that the songbird population is declining at an alarming rate. Quail, butterflies, bees, frogs, and many other creatures are disappearing way too fast. Shrinking islands of wilderness habitat are part of the problem, but traditional buffer zones in the rural and suburban landscapes are suffering, too, from human expansion. Vacant lots, wild fields, and hillsides transform quickly these days into vineyards, multilevel mansions, athletic fields, and office parks.

What we do with our piece of the planet counts more than ever. And what we do *collectively* to increase biodiversity may make the difference someday between abundant wildlife and none at all. Imagine corridors of backyard habitat gardens strung throughout backyards (and front yards), through parks and town centers. We may not be able to replicate nature on small lots, but we can create many different versions of mini-wildlife sanctuaries. The environmental costs of over watering, spraying, and fertilizing conventional landscapes have become a price too dear to pay. The alternative is a low maintenance, low-water use natural garden that feeds our souls while it nourishes local wildlife.

At our own pace in our own way, we can choose to go wild. Whether the focus is butterflies and birds or the full range of local wildlife, the effect is the same. In the process of creating sanctuary, the garden becomes something larger than its individual parts: it becomes habitat for people, plants, and animals. Along with it comes the unexpected and delightful discovery that something lovely, fun, and magical is also practical, easy, and environmentally sane.

50

APPENDIX

Host Plants for Common Butterflies of the San Francisco Bay Region
Including visitors and year-round inhabitants

California Buckeye • *Aesculus*
  • Spring Azure

California Coffeeberry • *Rhamnus*
  • Gray Hairstreak
  • Pale Swallowtail

California Lilac • *Ceanothus*
  • Spring Azure
  • California Tortoiseshell
  • California Hairstreak
  • Hedgerow Hairstreak

Creambush • *Holodiscus discolor*
  • Spring Azure
  • Pale Swallowtail
  • Lorquin's Admiral

Flowering Currants • *Ribes*
  • Tailed Copper

Oaks • *Quercus*
  • Spring Azure (Echo Blue)
  • California Sister
  • Mournful Duskywing
  • Propertius Duskywing
  • California Hairstreak

Willows • *Salix*
  • Western Tiger Swallowtail
  • Lorquin's Admiral
  • Mourning Cloak

Alfalfa, Vetch, Clovers, Lupines, Birds Foot Trefoil
  • Orange Sulfur (meadow habitat)

Bee Plant • *Scrophularia californica*
  • Chalcedon Checkerspot (found at higher elevations)

Buckwheats • *Eriogonum*
  • Acmon Blue
  • Purplish Copper
  • Green Hairstreak
  • Gorgon Copper (meadow & woodland edges)

Common California Aster • *Aster Chilensis*
  • Field Crescent

Dutchman's Pipe • *Aristolochia californica*
  • Pipevine Swallowtail (prefers riparian habitat)

Everlastings • *Gnaphalium., Anaphalis*
  • American Lady

Field Mustard • *Brassicas*
  • Sara Orangetip
  • Checkered White
  • Veined White
  • Cabbage White (Nasturtium)

Grasses • Carex
  • Grass Skippers
  • California Ringlet

Mallow • *Malvaceae*
  • Painted Lady
  • West Coast Lady
  • Common Checkered Skipper
  • Gray Hairstreak

Milkweed • *Asclepias*
  • Monarch

Plantain • *P. lanceolata; P. erecta*
  • Common Buckeye

Umbellifers
  • Anise Swallowtail

Nettles • *Urtica holosericea*
  • Satyr Anglewing
  • Painted Lady
  • Red Admiral (prefers riparian habitat; may also use Hops as host plant)

Passion Vine • *Passiflora*
  • Gulf Fritillary

Thistles • *Cirsium*
  • Mylitta Crescent
  • Red Admiral
  • Painted Lady

Wild Violets • *Viola*
  • Fritillaries

Care of Native Oaks

Oaks deserve special mention. Some experts consider them to be the most valuable wildlife habitat plants in California. Unfortunately, many people who have oaks on their property lose them by not understanding what they require to stay healthy. A native oak's natural conditions are winter rains and summer drought. Keep your native oaks healthy by following these guidelines.

Do not water mature oaks. Although it may take 10 years for a mature oak to die, frequent watering will eventually kill it. Planting under oaks and frequent irrigation cause root damage and stress.

When planting around and under oaks, use native shrubs, preferably, or other plants that require little or no watering. Contact the California Oak Foundation (510.763.0282) for their publication, Compatible Plants Under & Around Oaks ($12), or see their Web site: www.californiaoaks.org.

Minimize pruning.

Avoid cutting the roots; paving or trenching within the root zone, grade changes near the drip line, and soil compaction from parked cars, foot traffic, or construction.

Examine the base of the trunk. The tops of the roots should be visible near the trunk. Allow a thin layer of leaves around the base. Some experts recommend mulching with tree chips 3 to 6 feet from the base out to the drip line.

Habitat Gardening Help

Books & Field Guides
The California Landscape Garden • Mark Francis & Andreas Reimann
The Forgotten Pollinators • S. Buchmann & G. Nabhan
Gardening with a Wild Heart • Judith Larner Lowry
Grasses in California • Beecher Crampton
Growing California Natives • Marjorie G. Schmidt
The Landscaping Revolution • Andy Wasowski
The Natural Water Garden • (Brooklyn Botanic Garden Series)
Noah's Garden • Sara Stein
Noah's Garden: Restoring the Ecology of Our Own Backyards • Sara Stein
Plants of the San Francisco Bay Region • Kozloff & Beidleman
Water Conserving Plants and Landscapes for the Bay Area • Barrie Coate,
    (published by East Bay MUD)
Wild Gardens: A Living Legacy • Phyllis Faber

Common Butterflies of California • Bob Stewart
Common Dragonflies of California • Kathy Biggs
Good Bugs for Your Garden • Allison Starcher
Local Birds of the San Francisco Bay Area (Local Birds, Inc.)
Local Butterflies of the San Francisco Bay Area (Local Birds, Inc.)
National Geographic's Field Guide to the Birds of North America
The Orchard Mason Bee • Brian L. Griffin
Peterson's First Guide to Caterpillars • Amy Bartlett Wright

Habitat Gardens for Inspiration
East Bay Regional Parks Botanic Garden • Tilden Park, Berkeley 510.841.8732
The Gardens at Heather Farm • Walnut Creek 925.947.6712
Ardenwood Historic Farm • Fremont 510.796.0199
Native Plant Garden at Strybing Arboretum • San Francisco 415.661.3090
Richardson Bay Audubon Sanctuary • Tiburon 415.388.2524
Wildlife Habitat Garden at Harvest Garden for the Hungry • 1717 Yulupa
    Ave., Santa Rosa (open to the public)
The Butterfly Garden at Sonoma State University, Cotati, CA
Hallberg Butterfly Gardens • Sebastopol 707.823.3420

Plant & Wildlife Groups
California Native Plant Society 916.447.2677; email cnps@cnps.org
North American Butterfly Association (NABA) • North Bay Chapter;
    email NBAYButterfly@aol.com
Audubon Society/ California 916.481.5332
NWF Backyard Wildlife Habitat Program 707.790.4434

Advocates for Healthy Gardens
Garden Habitat Network • email jareimann@ucdavis.edu
  resource center for wildlife habitat creation and restoration
LifeGarden • Walnut Creek • 925.937.3044 *promotes ecologically friendly*
  gardens through education and community projects
Marin County Stormwater Pollution Program (MCSTOPP) • 415.499.6528
  less-toxic gardens, composting, insect guides for kids
Alameda Countywide Clean Water Program • 888.229.9473
Contra Costa Clean Water Program • 800.663.8674
University of California Cooperative Extension/Master Gardeners
  • Alameda County 510.639.1275 • Marin County 415.499.4204
  • Sonoma County 707.565.2608 • Contra Costa County 925.646.6540

Native Plant Nurseries
North Bay:
Larner Seeds • Bolinas 415.868.9407
O'Donnell's Nursery • Fairfax 415.453.0372
East Bay:
Berkeley Horticultural Nursery 510.526.5704
Native Here Nursery • Tilden Park, Berkeley 510.549.0211
Neglected Bulbs • Berkeley 510.524.5149
South Bay:
Native Revival • Aptos 408.684.1811
Yerba Buena Nursery • Woodside 650.851.1668
Sonoma County:
California Flora Nursery • Fulton 707.528.8813
Lone Pine Gardens • Sebastopol 707.823.5024 (mostly oaks)
Mostly Natives Nursery • Tomales 707.878.2009
North Coast Native Nursery • Petaluma 707.769.1213
Pond and Garden Nursery • Cotati 707.792.9141
Wayward Gardens • Sebastopol 707.829.8225
Western Hills Nursery • Occidental 707.874.3731

Internet Resources
Butterfly Encounters • www.butterflyfarm.com
California Native Plant Society • www.cnps.org
Common Dragonflies of California • www.sonic.net/dragonfly
Garden Habitat Network • www.gardenhabitat.net
Garden Web Native Plant Forum • www.gardenweb.com/forums/natives
Growing Native Research Institute • www.growingnative.com
LifeGarden • www.lifegarden.org
National Wildlife Federation • www.nwf.org
Nature Forum: The Wildlife Garden • www.nature.net/forums/garden
Wild Ones, Ltd. • www.for-wild.org

Plant Index